Spitting Image
THE GIANT KOMIC BOOK

I NOW DECLARE THIS BOOK OPEN

THIS IS INTERESTING, I'VE NEVER SEEN THE INSIDE OF A BOOK BEFORE

ROBERT Maxwell
THERE'S NOTHING HE CAN DO ABOUT THIS ONE!

AH – THE NEW SPITTING IMAGE BOOK HAS COME OUT– FIRE OFF SEVENTEEN WRITS IMMEDIATELY!

YOU CAN'T DO THAT...

WHY NOT?

BECAUSE ALL IT SAYS IS THAT YOU'RE A BIG FAT BLUBBERLIPS!!

WHERE?

JUST NOW

YOU'RE FIRED

...CONTINUED ON PAGES 84-93

The Lover

Geoffrey Howe's wet dream.

I often think it would be nice to have an imagination that ran away with me...

One that would make me run naked through golden fields of corn with Lady Howe...

Swing the mace about...

Drive down country roads in an open top sports car...

Make love on a beach with the surf swirling round me...

Join the Dangerous Sports Club...

That would make me disagree with Margaret Thatcher.

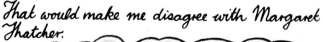

And the sort of imagination....

Core
processing

First Aid

INSIDE
SELLAFIELD
AN EXPLODED VIEW

Fission centre

Recycling plant

Cooling plant

Canteen

Reception

Tour buses

Tour

1 Piece that always goes wrong

2 This bit repaired with a bit of old Blue Tack and a couple of pieces from a Meccano set

3 Bucket of sand in case something goes wrong

4 Very important room where the Strontium A is turned to Strontium B (or was it the other way round. Oh shit, now I've forgotten)

5 Bit where they do exactly the same thing as they used to do at Chernobyl only this time they reckon it's safe

6 This one a bit wonky

7 This one decidedly wonky

8 One inch valve that keeps jamming

9 Bit where they throw the contaminated waste over the fence together with the grass clippings

10 Bit where all the dead fish have kept coming ashore for twenty years but we thought it was just a co-incidence

11 Very contaminated water

12 Very very very safe (for about ten seconds)

13 Lots of atoms in here (some safe)

14 The least safe of all the reactors

15 Mark I Ford Escort with jump leads attached in case they need to jump start the reactor

16 The safe bit (except when something goes wrong, when it isn't safe at all)

17 Video hire shop

18 Bit where the old Plutonium rods are stored in a Tesco carrier bag before the bin wagon comes round to collect them on a Thursday morning

19 This is the one we reckon will explode first

20 Room with monster chicken with ten heads

21 Frequent explosions in here

22 Only little explosions in here

23 This bit alright provided you keep the fag packet wedged in that socket to stop the thingy popping out and leaking radioactive isotopes everywhere

24 Lots of atoms in here

25 More atoms in here

26 Contaminated waste washed in the sink here

27 Contaminated waste flushed down the loo in here

28 Contaminated waste hidden under the carpet in here

29 Place where they go to get the hammer when the reactor keeps cutting out and they need to whack it

30 Bit where the contaminated waste is kept in a row of empty yoghurt cartons

31 This one used to have a roof till someone threw the wrong switch four weeks ago

32 Most people usually run past this building just in case it finally blows

33 This bit caught fire three times last week

34 This one could explode any second

35 Building that glows at night

36 This bit never really worked properly since we bought it from that second hand shop

37 Bit that has never worked properly

38 Bit that went up in flames last week and we didn't tell anybody

39 I wouldn't go in here unless you want all your hair to fall out

40 Main fuse box (with fuse removed and a paperclip used in its place)

41 Sorry, don't know what this one is

42 Nor this one

43 Nor this one either

44 Ah, now I think this may be the one where all the big bangs keep coming from

45 Rest room where we keep the table tennis table (only a bit radioactive)

46 Beach where the sand has just turned a nasty sort of brown colour and which made the dial shoot off the end of the scale on the Geiger counter

47 Bit where bathers come out of the water with a luminous lime green body

48 Meltdown likely to start here

49 Either the gents toilets or the main nuclear reactor, I'm not sure which

50 Pakistani newsagent

51 This bit bodged to get it to work

52 More atoms kept here

53 Lots of four feet rabbits with green ears in here

For the first time, a chance to see behind the barbed wire of the jewel in British Nuclear Fuel's crown, the Sellafield Atomic Energy Plant. How does it work? What makes it tick? When will it go off? Judge for yourself, as our artists lift the lid on Britain's foremost tourist detraction.

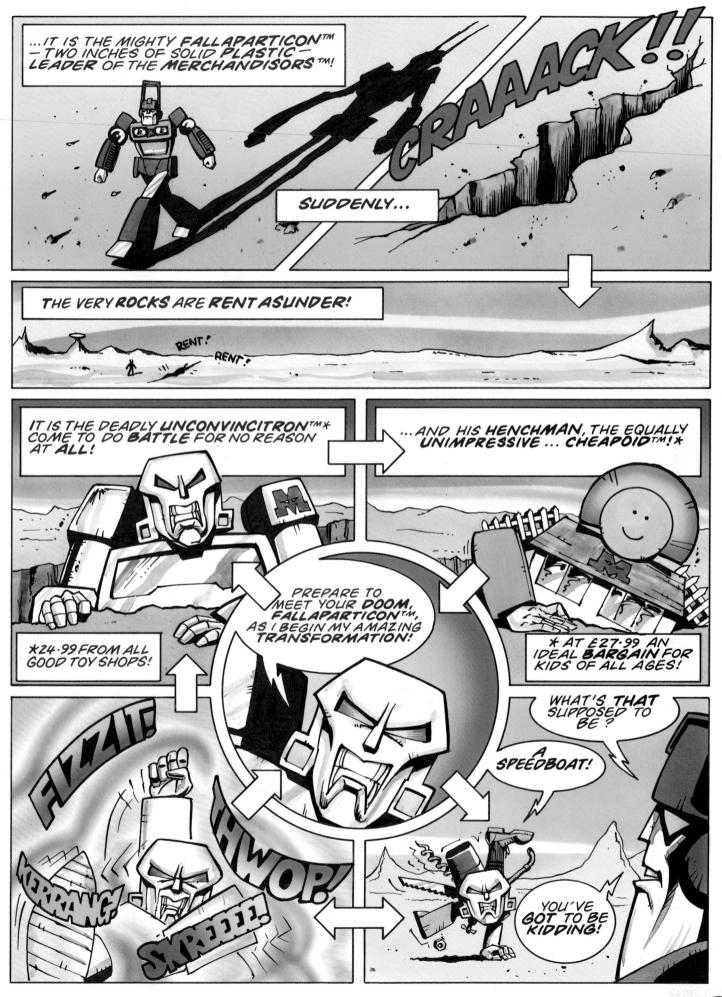

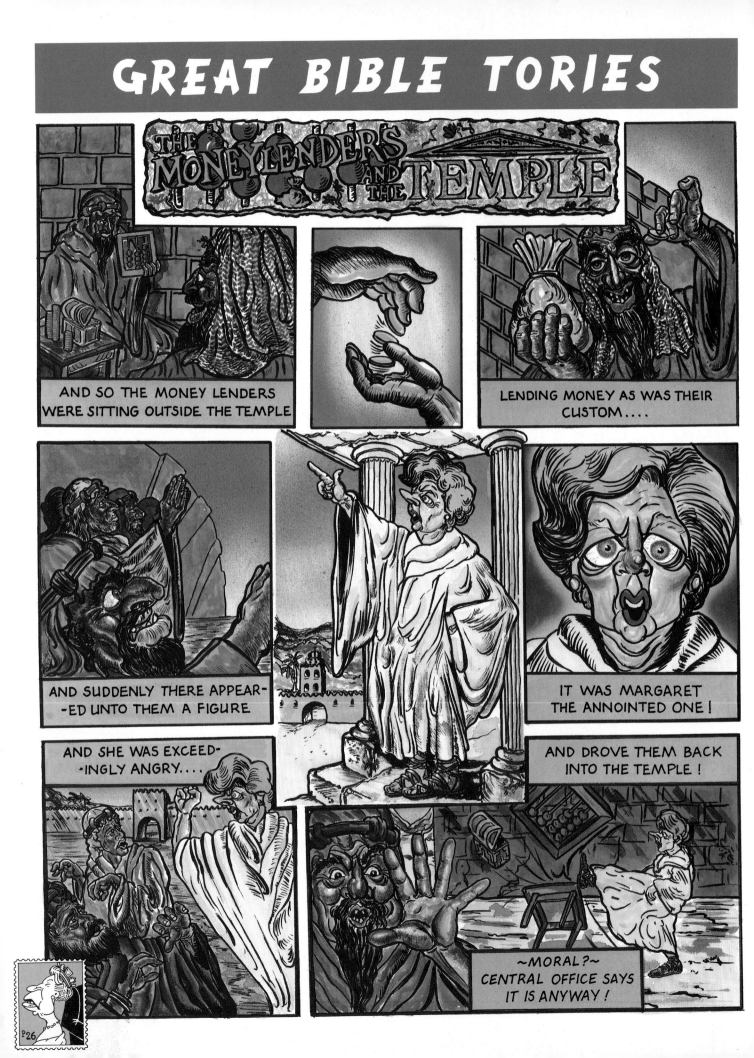

EMERGENCY EVACUATION

In the event of Ian Botham being a passenger on your flight, you should make yourself aware of the following emergency exits.

USE OF FIRE EXTINGUISHER

(Ian Botham only)

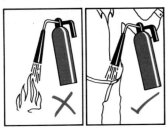

Insert knob B down fellow passenger's trousers then strike knob A to activate. Should fire extinguisher fail to work remove own knob and wave it about in your hands.

OXYGEN MASKS

(Ian Botham only)
Oxygen masks are provided in the case of decompression and should be used as a temporary jock strap.

SAFETY POSITION

Should it be necessary for Ian Botham to board the flight you should adopt the Emergency Safety Position shown.

IN FLIGHT MOVIE

(Ian Botham only)
During crucial scene(s) of the movie you should perform a hand shadow puppet in the shape of a large penis

in the centre of the screen.

LIFEJACKETS

(Ian Botham only)
Should be inflated while the flight is in motion, preferably as the air stewardess is walking past with the duty free trolley.

FASTEN SEAT BELTS

(Ian Botham only)
When the fasten seat belts light comes on you should get up, walk around, abuse the air hostesses, and empty the remains of your in-flight meal over Alan Border's head.

WONDERS OF THE WORLD   No. 9

ROBERT ROBINSON'S HAIR

Compared by ancients to the Hanging Gardens of Babylon, the Colossus of Rhodes and the Great Pyramid of Cheops, Robert Robinson's Hair has for centuries baffled scientists, mystics and astrologers. How long is it? Where does it come from? Where does it go to? The design of the hair is uncannily similar to the Labyrinth of the Minotaur designed by Daedalus and may perhaps have been inspired by the string that enabled Theseus to retrace his steps through the maze: forward and backward, round and round in circles, the Robinson Hair defies all known laws of gravity and dynamics.

The pattern as seen from the air has a distinct resemblance to some etchings of the mighty Peruvian Plain of Nazca. Is the hair some sort of beacon or landing strip for extraterrestrial beings or is the hair a religious symbol designed for worship of a great god in the sky? Or is it, as the wildest theories maintain, a rather feeble attempt to cover up a gleaming bald pate?

Perhaps we shall never know.

Only one thing is certain: Robert Robinson's Hair will remain for mother and youngest son of the Jones family from Hull quite the funniest thing they have ever seen.

Above: The Hanging Gardens of Babylon
Right: The Colossus of Rhodes
Below: Robert Robinson's Hair

P28

CONSTRUCT YOUR OWN

Cher, aged 35 and 9 yrs, is the glamorous star of films like **Moonstruck** and **Suspect**, and the theatre, like the one in Beverly Hills General Hospital. She had a hit record, **I Got You Babe** with her ex-husband **Sonny**, who enjoyed the experience so much he went into politics. They had a daughter, **Chastity**, made entirely out of scraps from Cher's first tummy tuck. Next week we show you how to make an evening dress just like Cher's out of an old satin posing pouch. And later in the *'chop-and-change'* series you'll have the chance to nip and tuck your own Nancy Reagan, Burt Reynolds and Victoria Principal.

CHER!

More defined cheekbones: **$13,000**

Sexy lips: **$8,500**

Larger breasts: **$18,000**

Double chin removal: **$4,000** (plus sales to Marlon Brando)

Rib removal: **$5,000** each (plus sales to Chinese restaurants)

Tummy tucks: **$20,000**

Pubic hair removal: **$6,000** (plus sales to cushion upholsterers).

Thigh defining: **$14,500**

NEXT WEEK
Construct your own Elizabeth Taylor, then marry her in Vegas . . .

Fingernails: **$900** each

High foot arches: **$3,000**

Calf curves: **$19,000**

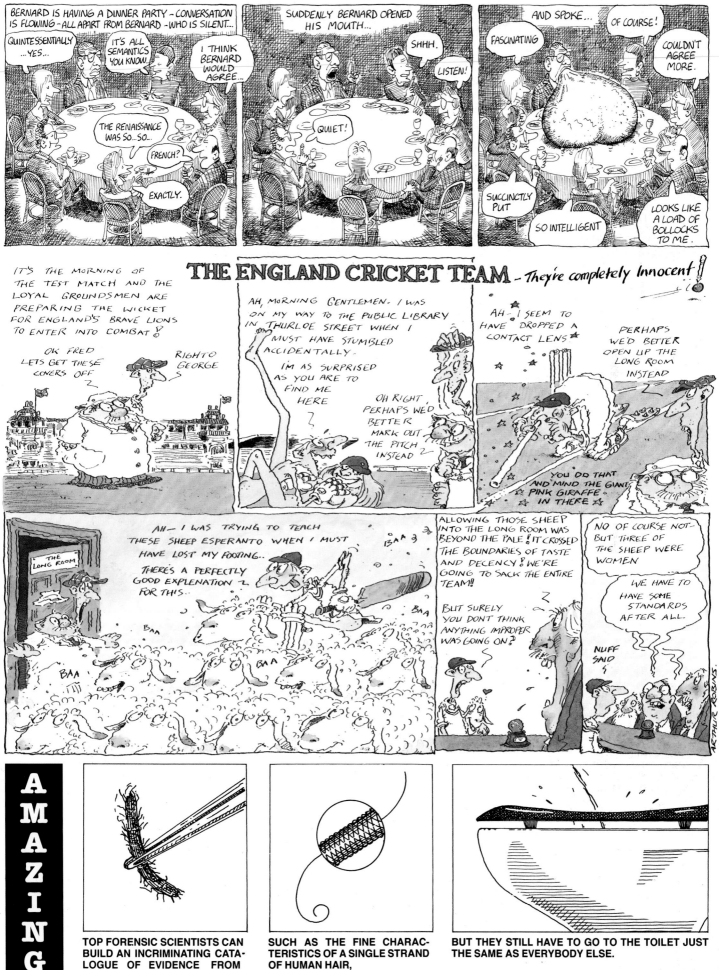

FERGIE WRITES:

Check your royalty quotient the Fergie way with my own foolproof **Royalometer**. Simply answer my questions, then check your score below to see how royal you are. Well go on then, off you go!

1 At a dinner dance you are offered a 'profiterole'. Do you?
a] Eat it
b] Ride it
c] Knight it
d] Troop it
e] Throw it

2 When introduced to a group of people you don't know, do you say?
a] And what do you do?
b] And what do you do?
c] D'you wear that tie for a laugh?
d] Turned out parky again ain't it!
e] Wotcha cock, gizza fag!!

3 The Queen's favourite pet animals are?
a] Corgis
b] Hamsters
c] Stick-insects
d] Gerry the Gerbil
e] Orville

4 Which of the following is not used regularly as a form of royal transport?
a] The Royal Train
b] The Royal State Coach
c] The Royal Skateboard
d] The Royal Yacht
e] The Royal Pogo-stick

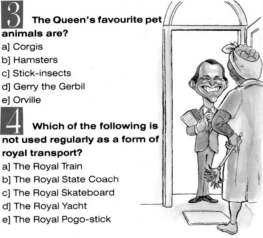

5 What does Princess Anne's husband do for a living?
a] He is a door-to-door encyclopaedia salesman
b] He is reserve left back for Torquay United
c] He is a farmer
d] He is the TV-am weather girl

6 What is the name of the Queen's youngest son?
a] Terry
b] Nobby
c] Edward
d] Jennifer
e] Thingy
f] Twithead
g] All of the above

7 What phrase did Prince Charles use to describe the proposed plans for the National Gallery extension?
a] A hideous and monstrous carbuncle
b] A complete and utter heap of old poo
c] A load of crap
d] The sort of thing I used to puke up at discos
e] Utter bollocks

8 Where does the Queen Mother live?
a] A semi in Walthamstow
b] Clarence House
c] Over the top of Ladbrokes

9 During the State Opening of Parliament by the Queen how does Black Rod gain entrance to the locked chamber of the House of Lords?

BATTLE

PICTURE LIBRARY

A BAYEUX PUBLICATION

No. 00001

PRICE ONE GROAT

CODENAME CONQUEST!

HASTINGS, THE SOUTH COAST OF ENGLAND 1066. ALL SEEMS QUIET, BUT THE THREAT OF INVASION HANGS HEAVY IN THE AIR ... TWO PLUCKY SAXONS SCOUTS BRAVELY SCAN THE HORIZON FOR SIGNS OF THE NORMAN BATTLEFLEET...

COR BLIMEY, NOBBY. NOW THAT OUR LIEGE HAROLD HAS PULLED A FAST ONE ON THAT FRENCHIE DUKE WILLIAM, THERE'S BOUND TO BE A BIT OF A SCRAP

NAH, DON'T YOU WORRY LOFTY. THEY SAY IT'LL ALL BE OVER BY MICHAELMAS. ANYWAY, I DON'T THINK THOSE FROGS'LL DARE SHOW UP

BUT EVEN AS HE SPEAKS MIGHTY FRENCH WAR MACH DRAWS EVER NEARER

DID YOU REMEMB TO BRING ZE GOLDE DELICIOUS?

DUTY FREE

P.42

a] He knocks three times on the door with his stick

b] He uses his spare key

c] He kicks the lock in with his Doc Martins

d] He pretends to be a flirtatious lady with no clothes on

e] He distracts the constable on duty by urinating in his pocket and slips past unnoticed when the officer looks round

10 When first introduced to the Queen you should address her as?

a] Ma'am

b] Your Majesty

c] Your Royal Highness

d] Darlin'

e] Mad Lizzie

f] Silly Old Moo

11 What make of vehicle did I drive before I got married?

a] A BMW

b] A Mark I Ford Escort with Magic Roundabout stickers on the doors

c] An ex-GPO Telecom van

d] A London Transport double decker bus

12 Where do the royal family do most of their shopping?

a] Harrods

b] Sainsbury's

c] Mr P.V. Patel's off-licence & tobacconist's

d] Car boot sales

13 What royal duty does my father perform?

a] He looks after Prince Charles's polo ponies

b] He looks after Prince Charles's polo mints

c] He mucks out Princess Michael of Kent

d] He is co-proprietor of the Bublos Kebab House in Edmonton High Road

14 Which of the following are not Princess Diana's favourite fabby pop group?

a] Dire Straits

b] Duran Duran

c] Paul Young

d] Herman's Hermits

15 To get into the Royal Enclosure at Ascot you must wear?

a] A hat

b] A horse

c] A jockey

d] A 'Royals Do It On A Red Carpet' T-shirt

16 If the Queen were to abdicate what would that make her?

a] The Queen Mother

b] The other Queen Mother

c] The Queen Mother-in-waiting

d] Mother to the Queen but Queen Mother's daughter

e] The Queen Mother's Daughter's Mother's Daughter's Mother

f] Very confused

17 Princess Margaret has a villa on which idyllic holiday island?

a] Mustique

b] The Isle of Wight

c] The Isle of Dogs

18 What subject did Prince Edward study at university?

a] Archaeology

b] Basket weaving

c] Car maintenance

d] Dressmaking

19 Where did Andy and I get married?

a] Westminster Abbey

b] Camden Registry Office

c] Ye Olde Smythe, Gretna Green

d] A Las Vegas 24-hr drive-in marriage chapel

20 At the Royal Film première what duties does the royal guest normally perform before the performance?

a] Gets the Ice creams in

b] Leads the catcalling and jeering during the adverts

c] Meets the performers

d] Has a big snogging session on the back seat of the stalls

21 Which of the following items of clothing are not suitable for a state banquet?

a] A pompon hat

b] Football socks

c] A kipper tie and 14" lapels

d] A tiara

22 At what sport did Princess Anne represent her country at the Olympic games?

a] Boxing

b] Synchronised swimming

c] Horse jumping

d] Shove ha'penny

Correct answers:

1. a & e 2. a & b 3. a & d 4. c
5. b & c 6. c, e & g 7. a, d & e 8. a
9. e 10. a, b, c & d 11. a & d
12. a & d 13. a & d 14. d 15. a & c
16. a, b, c, d, e & f 17. a & c 18. d
19. c 20. a, b, c & d 21. They are all suitable, well they are in my case 22. a, c & d

Score 5 points for every right answer. Deduct 5 points for every wrong answer.

200-215 Brilliant, you're Sir Alastair Burnet
150-199 Very good, you're either a royal or you've been cheating by looking at the answers.
100-149 Not bad, you might just about qualify for a ticket to a royal garden party.
50-99 Oh dear, no knighthoods for you I'm afraid.
under 50 Prince Edward

Eros was actually modelled on **Leon Brittan.**

Edwina Currie gave the kiss of life to an asthmatic goldfish in the middle of Piccadilly.

A creature from outer space once offered **David Steel** the job of Prime Minister of the Universe.

David Owen and the SDP are a new force in British politics

She could tell he was looking in her direction. Her heart beat faster. Surely he couldn't be going to speak to her. She was so ugly. It wasn't just her enormous head, her huge triangular nose, the small almond shaped eye set below her kidney bean ear. It was the way her arms came to a point. She supposed fingerless pointy hands were useful for opening cans of evaporated milk but that was all. She began to shed large surrealistic tears. But then she realised he was ugly too. His head must have been five times the size of his body, and his lips were at least three feet below his nose. He drew himself to his full height of one hundred and forty three centimetres and spoke.

"Hi, I'm a Radio Times illustrator." He divulged.

"And I illustrate for Vogue." She gasped.

They kissed as it rained pyramids.

THE END

THE CONQUERING DUKE WILLIAM CLAIMS THE CROWN OF ENGLAND!

AND, MEANWHILE, BACK ON A BEACH AT HASTINGS

CROWN THE BASTARD!

WHAT DO YOU ZINK OF ZE CROWN, JULES?

I'VE GOT JUST ZE TIE TO GO WIZ IT...

THERE'S GOING TO BE AN AWFUL BILL TO PAY

LOOKS VERY NICE ON YOU...

NORMAN SERVICE WILL BE RESUMED AS SOON AS POSSIBLE

So WILLIAM, YOU'VE GOT THE GRYPHON, THE FALCON, THE RAM, THE COFFEE PERCOLATOR, THE HI-FI, THE CROWN AND THE CUDDLY TOY... : DIDN'T HE DO WELL? :

SEE? I TOLD YOU IT'D BE OVER BY MICHAELMAS

For the FIRST time ever! The actual, ancient, old handbook THAT teaches heirs to THE throne how to BECOME king OR queen.

HOW TO BE THE QUEEN

CONGRATULATIONS! You are the new Queen. You have been chosen by a combination of divine right, a series of ancient European royal marriages and ... well ... luck ... to be the Queen of England and all that goes with it, like Fiji, well not Fiji actually but the other ones.

Some traitors would have it that your new job is easy. Well don't listen to them. It's dead hard. It's a bloody difficult job which you'll do bloody well.

The most important aspects of doing your bloody difficult job bloody well are listed below.

You must at all times be the following.

1 A CREDIT TO THE NATION

You achieve this by:

a] opening things
b] shaking hands with people
c] trooping the Colour
d] talking proper
e] opening things
f] being very nicely turned out indeed
g] sitting backwards on your horse
h] opening things
i] going to really hot countries, meeting strange foreigners, wearing dresses and not laughing
j] talking politely to great big fat ladies in white hats who make custard creams, no matter how incomprehensible they may sound to you
k] opening things

2 A TOURIST ATTRACTION

It is the historic duty of all those on whom the sacred responsibility of monarchy is bestowed to appear on mugs, tea-towels and postcards with 'Having a Regally Good Time' printed across the bottom.

3 A CONCERNED HEAD OF STATE

As a concerned head of state you will, from time to time, be required, at very short notice, to turn up and look serious at any or all of the following:

disasters, catastrophes, tragedies (inc. flash floods, hurricanes, sinkings, train/car crashes, explosions, severe cases of sunburn), hospitals, riots, plagues (both medical and of locusts), funerals of international bigwigs (deceased), mass anxiety attacks at Oxford Circus, Dutch Elm disease victims, the January sales, Preston v Bolton, Scotland, Dick's Donut Diner, Parliament.

4 AN ALL TOO LOVABLE MOTHER OF THE NATION

As an all too lovable mother of the nation you will, from time to time, be required, at very short notice, to turn up and look jolly at any or all of the following:

the Royal Variety Performance (yes, even when Tarby's on), children's hospitals, your Mum's birthday, any place where there are horses, airports in exotic locations swarming with Zulus, Aborigines, Welshmen.

N.B. It is very important not to mix up the above two.

Well that's about it really ... oh ... a few miscellaneous points.

A As the Queen you don't carry any money around with you, but you are entitled to carry around a copy of the Civil List. That should do the trick.

B On speaking to the public be very careful. Words that mean one thing to you very often mean something completely different to the general public. Below is a helpful list.

Word	Public's definition	Royal definition
Yacht	A boat with sails (10-25ft)	A floating palace (dead big)
Horse	Quadruped much used in sport	The Duchess of York
Equestrianism	Let's see what's on the other side	Brilliant
Home	Any ramshackle two-up, two-down that they can scrape enough money together to buy	Any one of a vast number of 200-roomed mansions, castles or palaces
Pr. Margaret	A lucky drunken old lotus eater	Your sister
Margaret Thatcher	That bitch in No. 10	That uppity bitch in No. 10

YOU ARE NOW THE QUEEN

EXCLUSIVE to this publication you won't see it anywhere else because it's only in this book no other book has a copy of it in libraries and shops all over the country if you want to see this exclusive publication you'll only see it in this exclusive publication in other words it's exclusive to this publication!

THE CHUNNEL: WO

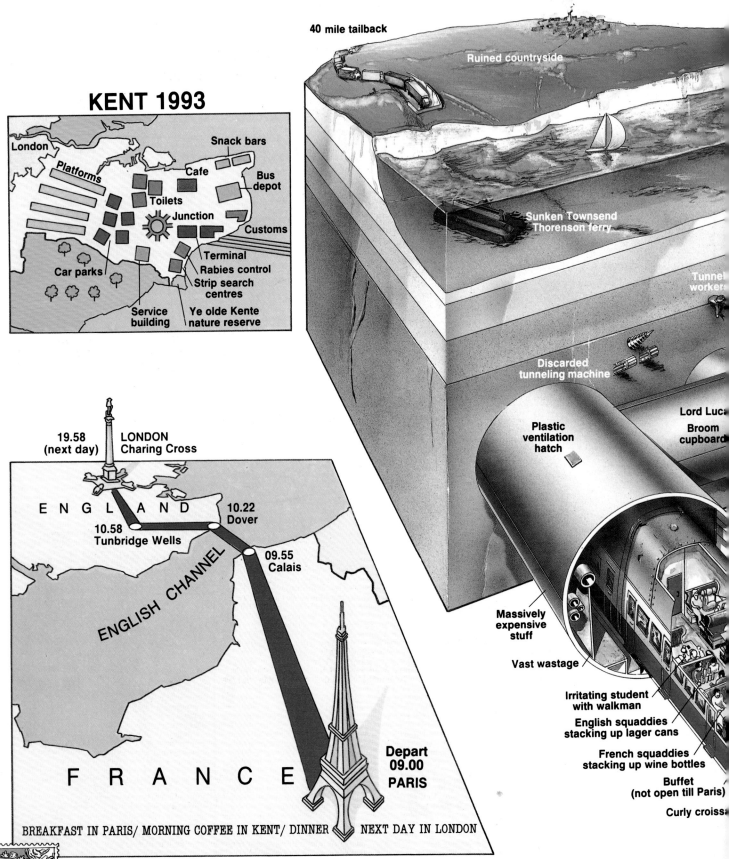

KENT 1993

- London
- Platforms
- Snack bars
- Cafe
- Bus depot
- Toilets
- Junction
- Customs
- Car parks
- Terminal
- Rabies control
- Strip search centres
- Service building
- Ye olde Kente nature reserve

40 mile tailback

Ruined countryside

Sunken Townsend Thorenson ferry

Tunnel workers

Discarded tunneling machine

Lord Luca Broom cupboard

Plastic ventilation hatch

Massively expensive stuff

Vast wastage

Irritating student with walkman

English squaddies stacking up lager cans

French squaddies stacking up wine bottles

Buffet (not open till Paris)

Curly croissa

19.58 (next day) — LONDON Charing Cross

E N G L A N D

10.22 Dover

10.58 Tunbridge Wells

ENGLISH CHANNEL

09.55 Calais

F R A N C E

Depart 09.00 PARIS

BREAKFAST IN PARIS/ MORNING COFFEE IN KENT/ DINNER NEXT DAY IN LONDON

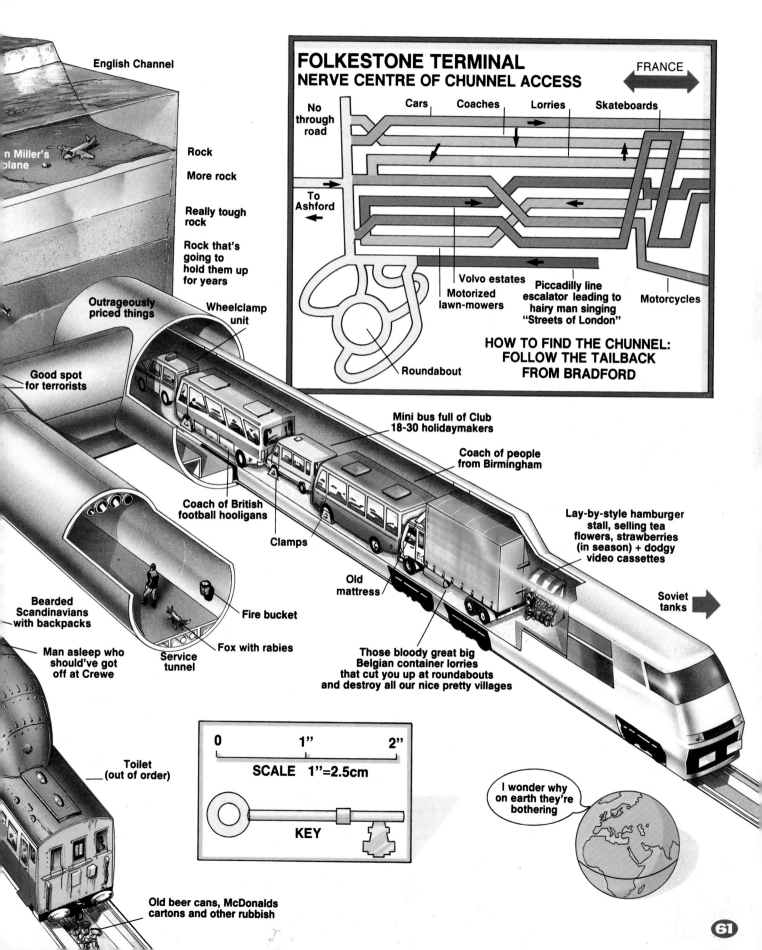

English Channel

n Miller's
plane

Rock

More rock

Really tough
rock

Rock that's
going to
hold them up
for years

Outrageously
priced things

Wheelclamp
unit

Good spot
for terrorists

Coach of British
football hooligans

Clamps

Bearded
Scandinavians
with backpacks

Man asleep who
should've got
off at Crewe

Fire bucket

Fox with rabies

Service
tunnel

Toilet
(out of order)

FOLKESTONE TERMINAL
NERVE CENTRE OF CHUNNEL ACCESS

FRANCE

No
through
road

Cars   Coaches   Lorries   Skateboards

To
Ashford

Volvo estates

Motorized
lawn-mowers

Piccadilly line
escalator leading to
hairy man singing
"Streets of London"

Motorcycles

HOW TO FIND THE CHUNNEL:
FOLLOW THE TAILBACK
FROM BRADFORD

Roundabout

Mini bus full of Club
18-30 holidaymakers

Coach of people
from Birmingham

Lay-by-style hamburger
stall, selling tea
flowers, strawberries
(in season) + dodgy
video cassettes

Soviet
tanks

Old
mattress

Those bloody great big
Belgian container lorries
that cut you up at roundabouts
and destroy all our nice pretty villages

0	1"	2"

SCALE   1"=2.5cm

KEY

I wonder why
on earth they're
bothering

Old beer cans, McDonalds
cartons and other rubbish

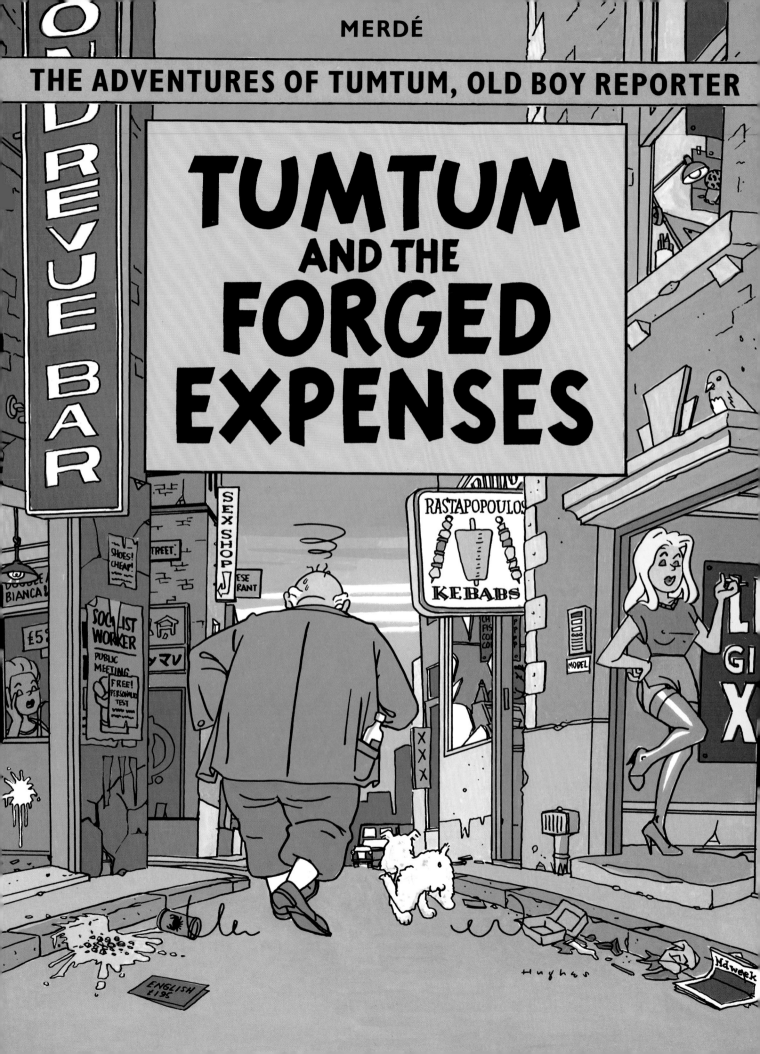

THE GROVELAGE ROYALE

For generation after generation of kings and queens of Europe the House of Burnet has descended . . . to its knees in abject servility. Now we can trace the historic lineage of this great cringing family, from humble fawners to even humbler fawners.

THE VENERABLE TOAD
The venerable toad worked by candlelight to chronicle his obsequious history of Anglo-Saxon England at all hours of the night. Toad sucked up to all the kings of the time and has gone down in history as "the first real genius of the English tongue".

DROOLIUS CAESAR
Friend of the more famous Julius Caesar who, on the Ides of March, repeatedly slapped him on the back.

POODEL
Loyal minstrel who searched throughout Europe for the imprisoned Richard I.

HAROLD HAHAHAHA-HARDRADA

SIR WALTER REILLEIGH – OBSEQUIOUS
Let Good Queen Bess walk all over him rather than get her feet wet

OLAF SOREKNEES

TUG FORELOCK
Led the so-called Pleasant's Revolt with a demand to give the monarchy more powers

LANCELOT DU LIC

MR CREPYS
London diarist who recorded the Great Fire of 1666 – and how wonderfully the King behaved throughout

SIR THOMAS MOREFLATTERY

THE DRIVELLERS
Obscure right-wing sect in 17th-century English politics

MR CREEPCRAWL
Dickensian character from 'Our Mutual Congratulation' based on the real 18th-century Mr Alastair Creepcrawl

KURT ZERUNDBOW
The Kaiser's wartime aide–de–camp

ALAIN ST BOWS LOTS
Possibly related to the Bowes Lyons'

MARECHAL NOSE
Napoleon's most faithful general

JOAN OF ARS
Martyr, burnt by the English for defending the Dauphin against his critics

MONSIGNOR PROSTRATE
Papal Nuncio to the court of Louis XIV, who he dubbed 'The Sun–shines–out–of–your–bottom King'

SIR ALASTAIR BURNET

LONGTONGUE
A companion of Falstaff and Pistol, Longtongue was a devoted friend to the young King Henry V. It was to Longtongue that Hal made his most stirring speech before Agincourt: "Once more unto my breeches, dear friend, once more." (HENRY V. III VII)

TURBANET
Turbanet was the official toady to the court of the Danish royal family of the 17th century. Shakespeare records his attendance on Prince Hamlet in the famous gravedigger scene of his play of the same name: "Alas, Turbanet, I knew him well." (HAMLET II. VII)

ALICE DE BURNETTE
Alice de Burnette was the foremost of the royal interviewers of the 1789 French Revolution. She never missed a day at the guillotine and conducted the last interview with the head of Marie Antoinette shortly after her death. It was to Alice that the doomed Queen made the remark, "Let them eat cake", to which Alice replied, "How tremendously amusing, Your Majesty, ha-ha-ha-ha."

JOHN BROWNNOSE
Queen Victoria's faithful Scottish attendant John Brownnose was much loved by his sovereign. Speaking playfully to him in French, she referred to him as "Brun-nez" and used his Scottish pet-name, Alastair. Alastair Brunette became his accepted title in the Royal Household, leading later to unkind stories about dyeing his hair. He died of a surfeit of humility during an interview with his Queen in 1897.

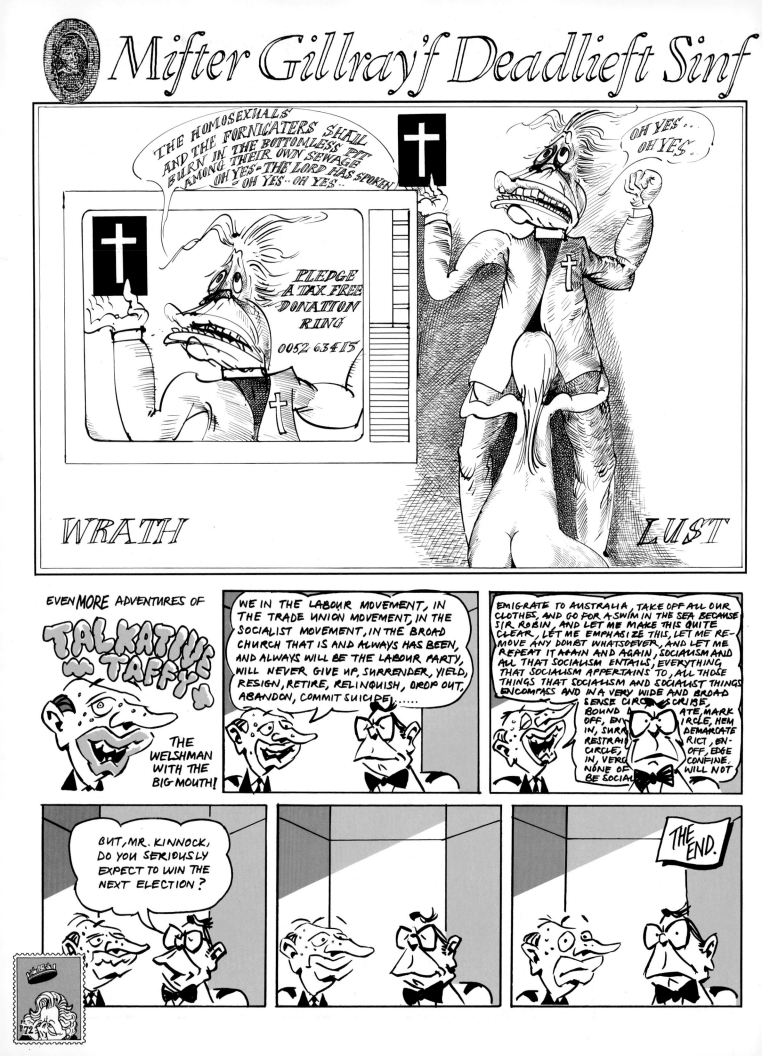

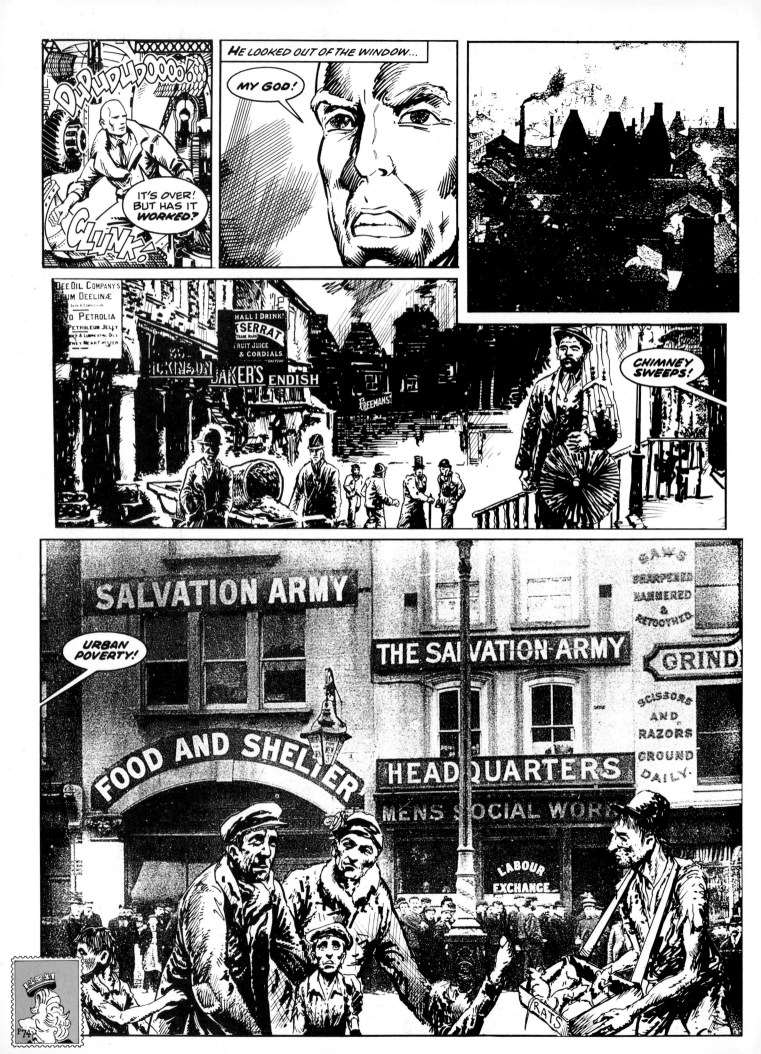

KEEPING AN ANIMAL AS A PET IN THE HOME CALLS FOR THE PROVISION OF THE CORRECT FOOD AND A SUITABLE CAGE. FOR EXAMPLE,

IT WOULD BE IMPRACTICAL TO KEEP A HAMSTER IN A MANILA ENVELOPE –

UNLESS IT HAD PREVIOUSLY BEEN INVOLVED IN A ROAD TRAFFIC INCIDENT.

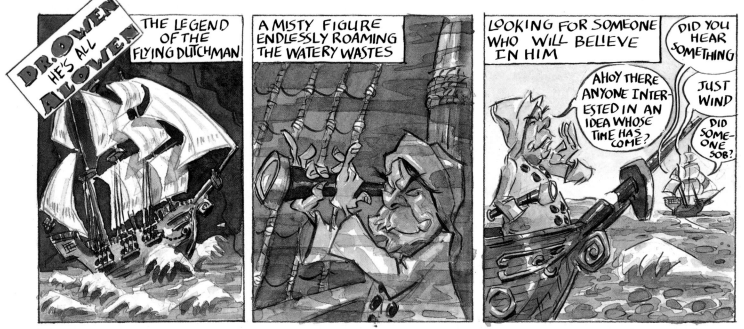

THE LEGEND OF THE FLYING DUTCHMAN!

A MISTY FIGURE ENDLESSLY ROAMING THE WATERY WASTES

LOOKING FOR SOMEONE WHO WILL BELIEVE IN HIM

DR. OWEN HE'S ALL ALOWEN

AHOY THERE ANYONE INTERESTED IN AN IDEA WHOSE TIME HAS COME?

DID YOU HEAR SOMETHING

JUST WIND

DID SOMEONE SOB?

WIMBLEDON: The Complete Coaching Course

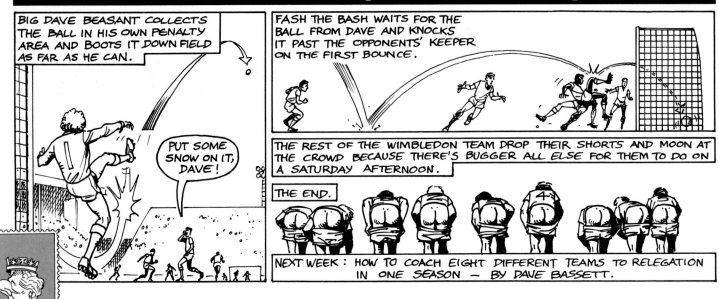

BIG DAVE BEASANT COLLECTS THE BALL IN HIS OWN PENALTY AREA AND BOOTS IT DOWN FIELD AS FAR AS HE CAN.

PUT SOME SNOW ON IT, DAVE!

FASH THE BASH WAITS FOR THE BALL FROM DAVE AND KNOCKS IT PAST THE OPPONENTS' KEEPER ON THE FIRST BOUNCE.

THE REST OF THE WIMBLEDON TEAM DROP THEIR SHORTS AND MOON AT THE CROWD BECAUSE THERE'S BUGGER ALL ELSE FOR THEM TO DO ON A SATURDAY AFTERNOON.

THE END.

NEXT WEEK : HOW TO COACH EIGHT DIFFERENT TEAMS TO RELEGATION IN ONE SEASON — BY DAVE BASSETT.

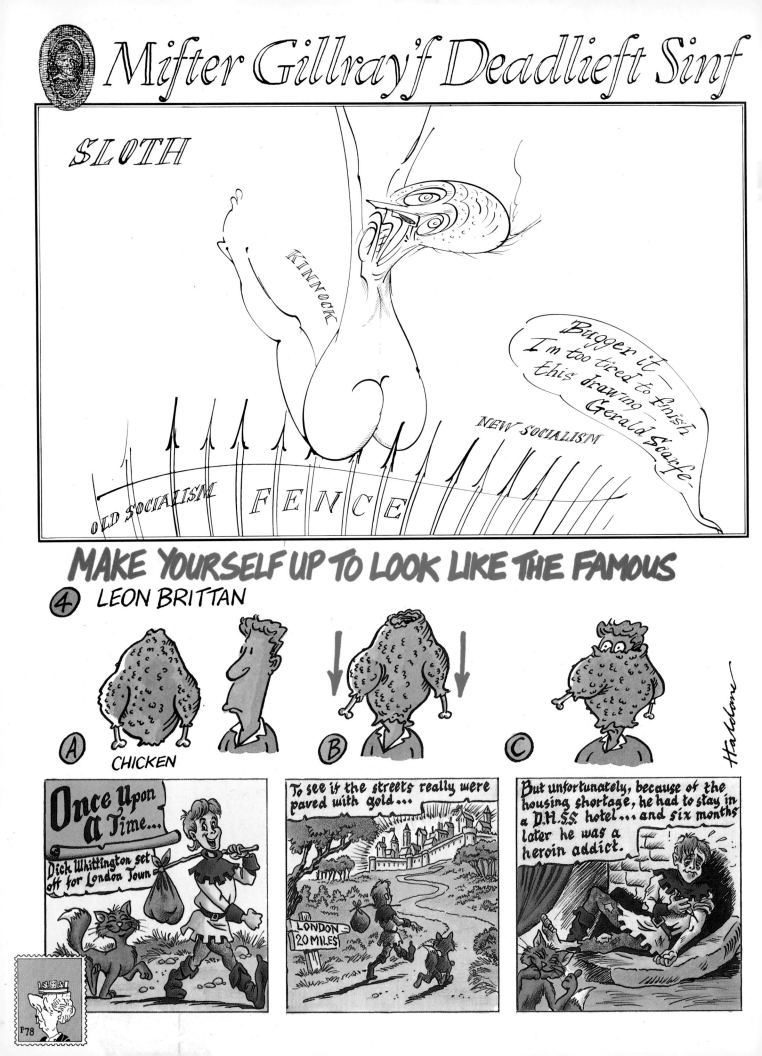

The IMPOSSIBLE Journey!

A Jeffrey Archer Adventure...

THE STORY SO FAR: **JEFF ARCHER**, INTERNATIONALLY RENOWNED NOVELIST, PLAYWRITE AND LITIGANT HAS BEEN SUMMONED TO THE OAK-PANELLED OFFICE OF **SIR BERNARD** — PERMANENT UNDER-SECRETARY AT THE DEPARTMENT OF UNDER-SECRETARIES.

I'm afraid there's a **problem** at the **seat of power!**

You mean № 10 Downing Street?

It's more fundamental than that...

PM's BOTTOM

I refer to the Prime Minister's **bottom**.

An unknown **obstacle** has blocked The Prime Ministerial **passage!**

With the vital East-West Summit coming up, The entire world could be plunged into almost certain total nuclear **doom!**

That's **ludicrous!** It could've come straight from one of my books!

We've tried everything: ex-lax, stewed prunes, chicken vindaloo— even hot **watney's.**

It seems the only answer is to **miniaturise** a crack squad of hand-picked operatives and send them into the PM's body in a **cheese** and **pickle sandwich!**

But... why **me**, sir? I'm only a bad novelist?

We **chose** you, Archer because... the trip could be a mite **tricky!**

What are our **chances?**

Optimistically speaking, you'll die...

...Along with your specially selected **crack team:** John Gummer, Cecil Parkinson, Edwina Currie and Sturmbannfuehrer Horst Von Spy!

Er, The intelligence boys tell us that one of the four is an **East German agent**— but the boffins have drawn a **blank** as to which one!

Rely on me, sir. If there's a Hun up the PM's Posterior, I'll soon flush him out

BOTTOM SECRET

So, thanks to the wonders of micro-technology and the free market, the S.S. EXPENDABLE and her valiant crew begin a perilous journey into— **the unknown!**

GULP!

BURP!

THE ART OF HORSEDRAWN CARRIAGE EVENTING

His Royal Highness Prince Philip explains

Mind your own bloody business

1. Jiggling harness
2. Whipple snaps
3. Pipcm rod
4. Futtock release
5. Grobbling tackle
6. Nibble spurglers
7. Whuming bit
8. Thong whanger
9. Slitty eyed Japanese tourist
10. Gobble protector
11. Ramplings
12. Fangle clods
13. Whip shankles
14. Niggle flange
15. Disappointing son who went into the wooftab biz
16. Bibnuts
17. Galipators
18. Clanking gear
19. 'Snodging pin
20. Fakkle sludge
21. Thong whanger
22. Gad
23. Bloody unemployed layabout shirker
24. Griddle scrum
25. Mattock weave
9. Distinguished oriental visitor. I was misquoted.
26. Tibbling sags
27. Dougs
28. Qnep nipper
9. He has got slitty eyes, though.
29. Carling flank
30. Panjandrum
31. Kernle spoke
32. Horse whip, for use on 23, 15, 9
33. Maggling tong
34. Scoffle
9. Bloody press misquoted me again! Very agreeable far eastern traveller. Not to be horse whipped at all.
23. Whipping's too good for this sort.
15. That doesn't apply to mincing, no-good nancy-boy son in the limp-wrist trade.
35. Clunt whuppler
36. Nadger
37. Buggle buntlock
38. Pog strimping
9. Look, it's a genetic fact — he has got slitty eyes
39. Cobble grudger
40. Bigot

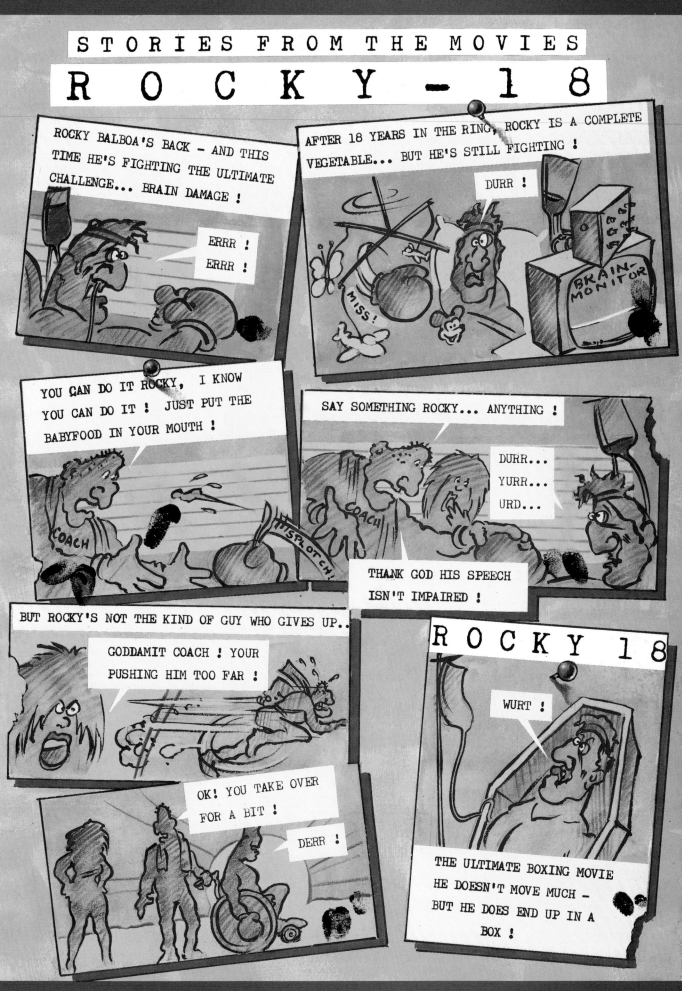

T-shirts for two

Be a strutting style warrior with these fabulous Spitting Image designer T-shirts. Straight from our London fashion studio, these exclusive off-the-peg creations come in two outstanding designs: The Sporting Image sweat top, and the Giant Komic Book T-shirt. They'll put heirs on your chest — or give you a Prime Ministerial cover-up!

SWEAT TOP

Designed exclusively for the **Spitting Image Komic book** and featuring the great Komic panel sewn onto a heavyweight fleece. The fashionable Sweat Top is made of 100% cotton and features a zip neck and drop shoulders. The Top is available in black only and comes in two generously cut sizes: X-Large for men, Medium for women.
Price: £24.99 (Including postage and packing per item)

T-SHIRT

Available in white **high quality 100% premium cotton** and featuring a colourful Komic print. The T-Shirts are available in two baggy sizes: X-Large size for men and women and a **youth** size.
Price: £7.99 (Including postage and packing per item)

Style	To Fit Chest Size	Price
X-Large Sweat Top	40-44 inches	£24.99
Medium Sweat Top	34-38 inches	£24.99
X-Large T-Shirt	34-44 inches	£7.99
Youth T-Shirt	30-32 inches	£7.99

HOW TO ORDER

To order the Sweat Tops and T-shirts please write clearly stating your name, address, telephone number and requirements including the size(s) required.
Make your cheque or postal order (no cash, please) payable to **Spitting Image Distributions** and send to:
**Spitting Image Distributions
PO Box 437
N2 Metropolitan Wharf
Wapping Wall
London E1 9TT**
(Please put your name and address on the back of your cheque).
Alternatively Barclaycard and Access cardholders may order by telephoning our credit card line on 01-480 7690 – (Orders only – This is not an enquiry line). Your account will be debited when your purchase is sent to you.

Your garments should be received within 28 days of receipt of order. The offer is open only to readers living in Great Britain and Northern Ireland and remains open until the 31st January 1989. If you are not entirely satisfied, please return within seven days with a covering letter and your money will be refunded in full. We cannot be held responsible for returned goods lost in transit. The colours are as accurate as the printing process allows.

P96

EDITED BY:

Nick Newman, except for the last two blatently capitalist, money grabbing, greed ridden pages

John Kelly
Roger Law
Juliette Walker
Special thanks to **Escape Magazine** and to **Steve Dillon**

DESIGNED BY:

Alex Evans

PRODUCED BY:

David Bann
Anne Cartwright
Clive Frampton

WRITTEN BY:

Geoff Atkinson
David Austin
Banx
Michael Barfield
Steve Bell
Marcus Berkmann
Mark Brisenden

John Docherty
David Haldane
Ian Hislop
Moray Hunter
Guy Jenkin
John O'Farrell
Nick Newman
Ged Parsons
Geoffrey Perkins
Ken Pyne
Tony Sarchet
Paul Simpkin
Andrea Solomons
Harry Thompson
Mark Warren
Kipper Williams

DRAWN BY:

Jos Armitage (Ionicus) Prof. Brainstorm
Neville Astley Animated stamp
Steve Bendelack Money lenders
Steve Bell Heaven
Banx Mrs. Macartney, They came from outer space
Pablo Bach Cher, Network 7, Weathermen, Robert Robinson, Memory loss, Sitcom, Schwarzenegger, Fat and useless, Charles and Di, Waldheim, How royal, Sheens
Rowen Clifford Howe's wet dream
Paul Cemmick Noel Edmunds, Fat chats, On the couch, Two gun Ron
Simon Cooper Prof. Pessary
Steve Dillon God, Receivers, Wimbledon, Annabel Croft, Bowls, Sumo, Garden beautiful
Mark Draisey Cinderella, Moggy, Jagger
Hunt Emerson Howe's bad dream
Brett Ewins Week in politics, Beirut Force, Judge Deaf
Charles Griffin Doris Stokes
Phil Gascoigne Dr. Finley
Colin Hadley Amazing
David Haldane Oliver Reed, Look famous

Ryan Hughes Tum Tum
David Hughes Face masks
John Higgins Not much cop
Graham Humphries John Hurt, Death Wish, Rocky, Bruno
Tony Joswick Stranger than fiction
Ian Jackson Terry's toupée
Johnny Johnstone 'Killer' Killer
John Lawson and Geoff Sims Chunnel, Sellafield
Sophie Law Prince
Harry North Impossible journey, The druggies
Tony McSweeney Bayeaux tapistry
Charles Peattie Talking Bollocks
Arthur Robbins Cricket, Kissogram
Lee Sullivan Merchandisers
Paul Sample Major Fergie, Horsedrawn carriage
Neville Smith Frank Bough
Gerald Scarfe Deadly sins
Paul Slater Grovelage royale
Paul Stone Dick Whittington, Rumpelstiltskin
David Stoten Taffy, No head Robson, Pomposity on two, Fortress Wapping, Cecil Maxwell, Runcies, Johnny one joke
Graham Thompson Ridley
Janet Woolley Short story
Tim Watts Political facts, Dr. Owen
John Watson Glasnost
Oscar Zarate Rentaquote, Jacko

LETTERED BY:

Ali McKay 'Killer' Killer, Stranger than fiction, Not much cop
Richard Starkling Merchandisers

COLOURED BY:

Tom Frame Heaven
Clive Frampton Horsedrawn carriage

COVER BY:

David Stoten, John Burns and **Alex Evans**

Published in 1988 by Pyramid Books an imprint of The Octopus Publishing Group, Michelin House, 81 Fulham Road, London SW3 6RB

Copyright © 1988 Spitting Image Productions Limited

ISBN 1 871307 48 1

All rights reserved. No part of this publication may be reproduced, stored in a retrieval system, or transmitted in any form or by any means, electronic, mechanical, photocopying, recording or otherwise, without the permission of The Octopus Publishing Group

Printed in Great Britain by ALLAN-DENVER

SENT ON AN INTERCITY SAVER TO OBLIVION BY 'KILLER' KILLER OF THE SAS

Er... well... ..HELLO.. Good evening... ..and WELCOME, to what promises to be ....THE END!

Fool your friends with these **amazing** Spitting Image Komic Nose, Tongue and Eye Masks!

FREE!

STUNNING!

Simply cut round the dotted lines, and **BINGO!** With the Queen on your hooter, you'll suddenly be having 5,000 people round for tea! With your tongue slavering out of Sir Alastair's mouth, you'll be the Newscaster Laureate in no time! And wearing Michael Caine's glasses, you'll be playing Michael Caine in the new Michael Caine film! Yes, you'll have decades of fun — and more faces than even Neil Kinnock!